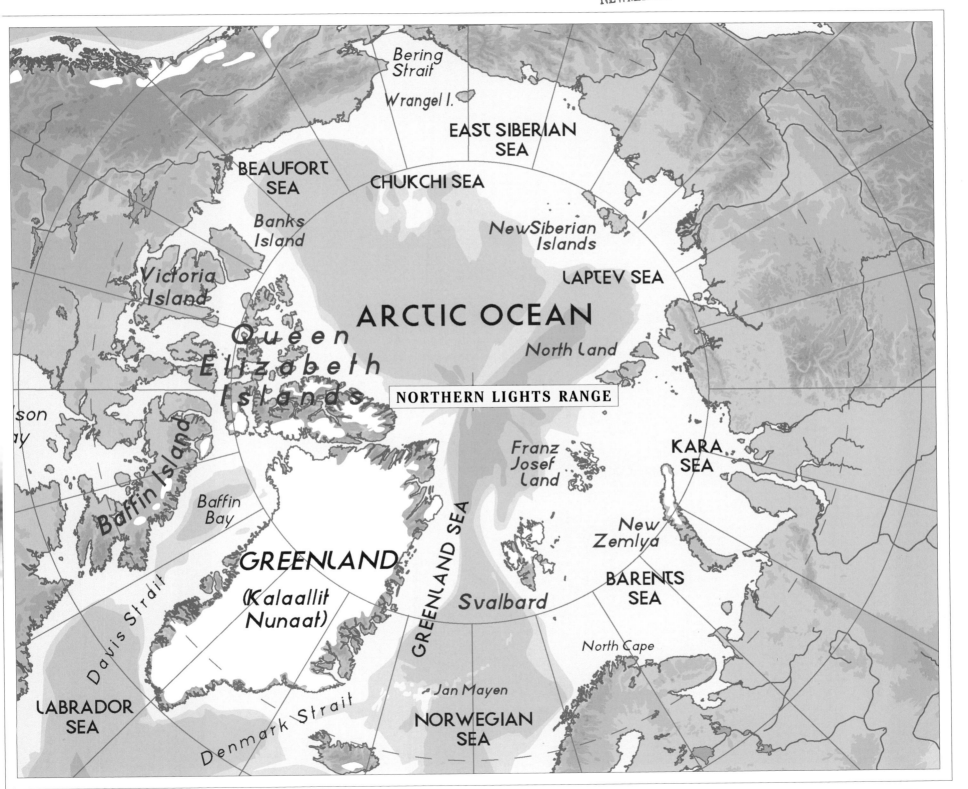

Bering
Strait

Wrangel I.

EAST SIBERIAN
SEA

BEAUFORT
SEA

CHUKCHI SEA

Banks
Island

New Siberian
Islands

Victoria
Island

LAPTEV SEA

Queen

ARCTIC OCEAN

North Land

Elizabeth

Islands

NORTHERN LIGHTS RANGE

son
ay

Baffin Island

KARA
SEA

Franz
Josef
Land

Baffin
Bay

GREENLAND

New
Zemlya

Davis Strait

(Kalaallit
Nunaat)

GREENLAND SEA

Svalbard

BARENTS
SEA

North Cape

LABRADOR
SEA

Jan Mayen

NORWEGIAN
SEA

Denmark Strait

Published by Creative Education
123 South Broad Street
Mankato, Minnesota 56001

Creative Education is an imprint of The Creative Company.

Designed by Stephanie Blumenthal
Production design by The Design Lab

Photographs by Corbis (Archivo Iconografico S.A., Bjorn Backe; Papilio, Bettmann, Burstein Collection, Dennis di Cicco,
Macduff Everton, Hulton-Deutsch Collection, Images.com, Lake County Museum, Danny Lehman, George D. Lepp,
Michael Maslan Historic Photographs, Digital image © 1996 CORBIS; Original image courtesy of NASA, Gianni Dagli Orti,
Gabe Palmer, Carl & Ann Purcell, Roger Ressmeyer, Jim Richardson, Royalty-Free, Masahiro Sano, Paul A. Souders, Stocktrek,
Kennan Ward, Ron Watts), Geoatlas/World Vector 3 Map CD, Minneapolis Public Library, Minneapolis Collection,
NASA/ESA; John Clarke (University of Michigan), National Oceanic and Atmospheric Administration (NOAA) Photo Library;
Historic NWS Collection, The Nobel Foundation

Printed in the United States of America

Library of Congress Cataloging-in-Publication Data

Kalz, Jill.
Northern lights / by Jill Kalz.
p. cm. — (Natural wonders of the world)
Summary: Discusses the auroras, or northern lights, presenting information on
their causes, characteristics, and some historical and folkloric references to them.
ISBN 1-58341-326-X
1. Auroras—Juvenile literature. [1. Auroras.] I. Title. II. Series.

QC971.4.K35 2004   538'.768—dc22   2003065231

First edition

2 4 6 8 9 7 5 3 1

NORTHERN LIGHTS

JILL KALZ

CREATIVE EDUCATION

POWERED BY THE SUN

They dance to their own music, to songs older than Earth itself. Wide, translucent ribbons of colored light furl and unfurl across the night sky—one moment slow and billowing, the next snapping like a cracked whip. Although science explained the mechanics of this wonder decades ago, human imagination and spirit have always breathed a sense of magic into it. Scientifically

known as the *aurora borealis* ("northern dawn"), the luminous display is more commonly called the "northern lights."

The northern lights are a **celestial** phenomenon that occurs over the northernmost regions of the earth, including Alaska, Canada, Greenland, Iceland, and the northern tips of Norway, Sweden, Finland, and Russia. Seen from space, the northern nights form a lopsided ring roughly centered on Earth's **geomagnetic north pole**. This ring, called the auroral oval, remains more or less fixed in space with reference to the sun while the planet tilts and rotates below it. As a result, the viewing area for the

An aurora also exists in the southern hemisphere, its oval encompassing most of Antarctica. Called *aurora australis*, or the "southern lights," this aurora is a much rarer sight, as it occurs mostly over uninhabited regions. Displays occur simultaneously, mirror image-like, with those of the northern lights.

5

The solar wind blows so fast that it usually takes fewer than 48 hours for it to travel from the sun to Earth—a distance of 93 million miles (150 million km)! When solar activity is at its peak, solar winds can reach Earth in a day.

Violent eruptions on the surface of the sun are the power source for the northern and southern lights.

northern lights changes from hour to hour, and from season to season. Anchorage, Alaska, for example, may be directly below the oval at 6 A.M. but completely out of it by 6 P.M.

Although most visible around midnight, in varying degrees of brightness, the northern lights dance day and night, every day of the year. It is impossible to see them with the naked eye during the day, however, because their light, like that of the stars, cannot outshine the sun's brilliance.

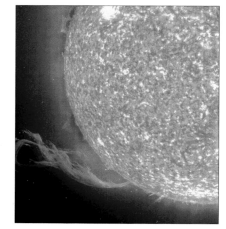

Power for the northern lights comes from the sun. The heat generated within the sun is so intense that it is continually breaking apart the gases of which the sun is made, creating a hot "soup" of atomic particles. Atoms are the tiny building blocks of which everything in the universe—solid, liquid, or gas—is made. They are so tiny that millions of them would fit inside the period at the end of this sentence. But as small as they are, atoms can be split into even smaller parts

6

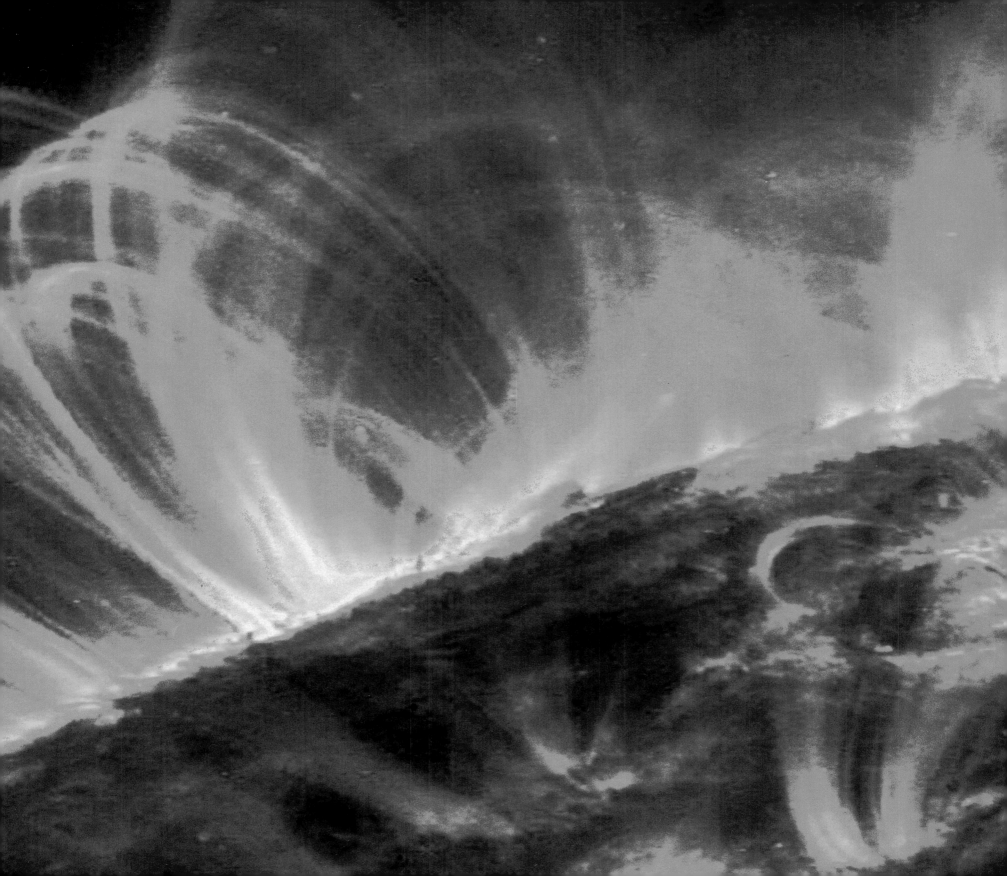

Like Earth, Jupiter (opposite) is protected from damaging solar particles by an invisible magnetic field, colored blue in this photo (right) for illustration purposes.

called protons, neutrons, and **electrons**. And it is these atomic particles that are forcefully blown away from the sun's surface as the solar wind.

Traveling at speeds between 300 and 600 miles (480–970 km) per second, the solar wind blows nonstop in all directions. As it approaches Earth, it encounters the planet's comet-shaped **magnetic field**, which serves as a protective shield. Most of the solar particles flow around

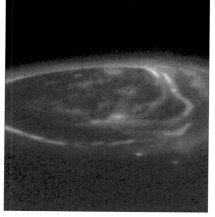

this shield, but some slip through it and become electrically charged. Like a giant bar magnet, Earth pulls these particles to its north and south poles, where the magnetic attraction is strongest. There the solar particles enter Earth's **atmosphere** and collide with the atoms and **molecules** of the atmosphere's gases. The energy created by each collision is released as light—the light of the **aurora**. In the northern hemisphere, this aurora is known as the northern lights.

8

Earth isn't the only planet with auroras. As long as a planet, or any celestial body, has an atmosphere and a magnetic field, it can experience auroras. Planets Jupiter, Saturn, Uranus, and Neptune have auroras, as do some of their moons, such as Saturn's Titan and Neptune's Triton.

SHAPES, COLORS, AND WHISPERS

The chances of seeing the northern lights decrease as one moves farther south. People in Greece, for example, witness displays only once every 100 years on average. Rarer still are auroral displays over the equator, which usually appear just once every 200 years.

While scientists tried to dissect the processes behind the northern lights, poets such as Bayard Taylor (right) celebrated the lights' mystery in verse.

No two northern lights displays look exactly the same. One night, the lights may arch across the sky, their lower edge sharply defined, their upper edge erupting into tall columns. The next night, they may hang quietly in curtains of color. They may start as one shape but transform into another a few seconds later. American poet Bayard Taylor (1825–78) described the northern lights he once saw as a "scarf of silver fire stretching directly across the zenith. . . . Presently it began to waver, bending back and forth, sometimes slowly, sometimes with a quick, springing motion, as if testing its elasticity."

Even though each display is unique, several shapes occur regularly. Early scientists assigned to them names such as "arc," "band," and "ray." While the terms are still used by amateur observers, scientists no longer have much use for them. More interested in the invisible processes that create the northern lights than the lights' physical appearance, researchers today rely on satellites and computer technology rather than observations with the naked eye.

Auroral colors vary according to the types of gas atoms or molecules with which the solar particles collide. High-altitude oxygen atoms burn a deep red. Lower-altitude oxygen atoms glow yellow-green. Rare low-altitude pink and blue-violet auroras are caused by nitrogen molecules. The strength of the incoming solar particles

The inconsistency of northern lights displays is arguably their most intriguing quality. They never appear exactly the same way twice. Their shapes, colors, and locations depend on a number of factors, including the intensity of solar activity, tilt of Earth, and the presence of particular atoms and molecules.

Auroral stories share common themes but differ in the details. The Chippewa Indians once believed that the northern lights signaled a successful hunt. To people in central Asia, they represented birth and fertility. People in Finland believed they were seeing silver-coated foxes sprinting across the night sky, sparks flying from their fur.

determines how far into the atmosphere they will travel. Low-energy particles, for example, will be able to penetrate only the upper level of the atmosphere and will therefore collide with high-altitude oxygen atoms, creating all-red auroras. Auroras shine brighter as the number of solar particles streaming into the atmosphere increases.

It may often look as though the lower edge of the northern lights, like the ends of a rainbow, is touching the earth, but it usually lies no closer than 60 miles (97 km) above the ground. That's more than 10 times higher than the cruising altitude of most passenger jets! And the upper edge may extend as high as 620 miles (1,000 km)! Curiously, despite this distance, some people claim to have actually *heard* the northern lights. They describe the sound as "swishing" in time with the aurora's

movements or "crackling." Scientists say this is unlikely, because the atmosphere in which the lights dance cannot support sound waves. Even if it could, there would be a delay between the aurora's movement and the sound it makes, like the delay between a flash of lightning and thunder.

Some researchers suggest that the "swishing" sound may actually come from inside an observer's head—that the brain may be mistakenly translating visual signals into audio ones. The "crackling" sound may be the result of built-up static electricity in the air or vibrations in objects such as trees and rocks caused by aurora-induced electrical currents. But no one has successfully recorded the sounds of the northern lights, so for now, its "whispers" remain a mystery.

Scientists use the delay between thunder and lightning to refute claims made by casual observers (and many ancient legends) that the northern lights "crackle" as they move. Light waves travel through the atmosphere at a much greater speed than sound waves, so a flash of lightning is always seen before it is heard. It is impossible for them to occur simultaneously.

Skylab (above) was the United States' first space station, an orbiting laboratory that, among other things, allowed astronauts to gather a huge amount of data about the sun. This information gave scientists a new look at how solar activity affects Earth's weather and phenomena such as the northern lights.

One of the most common shapes for the northern lights to assume is an arc with rays (left). This shape occurs frequently during times of moderate to high solar activity. The arc stretches across the sky from east to west, and its rays, following the earth's magnetic field, dance upon it.

PUZZLES IN THE SKY

"Talking back" to the northern lights is encouraged by some cultures, as the lights are seen as messengers of the spirit world. But in many others, it is said to be deadly. Some Inuits say that whistling at the aurora will cause it to swoop down and cut off one's head!

Over thousands of years, the human imagination has turned the northern lights into animal spirits, marching armies (opposite), and much more.

Because the northern lights are as old as Earth itself, it's impossible to know exactly who saw them first. But it was certainly a member of one of the **indigenous** peoples of the northern regions, as all of them tell auroral stories that have been passed down through the generations.

The **Inuit** people have lived beneath the northern lights for more than 6,000 years. Some villages believe the lights are torches lit by the spirits of the dead to guide new arrivals to heaven. Others believe that the souls of their favorite animals—deer, whales, seals, and fish—dance in the flickering light. One legend claims that the northern lights are spirits playing soccer with a walrus or human skull. Supposedly, their feet can be heard crunching in the heavenly snowfields.

While folk tales were plentiful throughout the northern regions of the world, and polar explorers wrote memoirs about and painted pictures of the aurora, science made little progress in explaining the workings of the northern lights until the 1870s. At that time, researchers discovered a correlation between large numbers of **sunspots**, changes in Earth's atmosphere, and intense northern lights displays. But no one knew why the correlation existed—until Norwegian researcher Kristian Birkeland offered an explanation.

Often referred to as the "father of modern auroral science," Birkeland suggested that electrons blown from sunspots were pulled into Earth's magnetic field, triggering auroras. He constructed a model in which a magnetized globe (representing Earth), suspended in

Intrigued by the work of Kristian Birkeland and the auroral photography of Carl Størmer, Swedish physicist Hannes Alfvén (right) was one of many who attempted to explain the origins of the northern lights during the first part of the 20th century—and he succeeded, receiving the Nobel Prize in Physics for his efforts. He died in 1995.

a near-vacuum (Earth's atmosphere), was bombarded with electrons (solar wind). As he predicted, rings of light began to glow around the globe's poles. Birkeland announced his findings at the turn of the 20th century, but to his astonishment, the scientific community largely rejected his conclusion, still unconvinced that solar particles could reach and penetrate Earth's atmosphere. After Birkeland's death in 1917, his work was taken up by fellow Norwegian Carl Størmer, who by the end of his career would shoot more than 40,000 auroral photographs and find a way to calculate the auroral heights.

Other researchers continued to puzzle over the northern lights' origin as well, but it was Hannes Alfvén, a young Swedish physicist, who revisited Birkeland's findings, recalculated, and presented the auroral theory accepted today as fact. Alfvén, like Birkeland, initially had trouble convincing the scientific community. However, whereas Birkeland had no way of proving many of the things about which he theorized, Alfvén benefitted from the introduction of satellite and rocket technology. In the early 1960s, measurements taken from space at last confirmed the presence of the solar wind, Earth's magnetic field, and the sun's role in aurora creation. In part for his pioneering work in auroral science, Alfvén was awarded the Nobel Prize in Physics in 1970.

Before the 19th century, some scientists believed that the northern lights were reflections off polar ice. Others thought they were fires in distant oceans. Still others claimed that stray beams of sunlight slipped past the curve of the earth and lit the night sky.

The advent of satellite technology in the early 1960s finally allowed scientists to confirm what early researchers had long theorized about aurora creation. Dishes such as this one captured data sent by satellites in orbit.

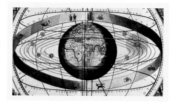

IN ANOTHER 11 YEARS

Because displays in central and southern Europe were rare and usually red (as they still are today), early Europeans feared bloody wars were being waged above them and saw the aurora as a sign of the **apocalypse**. People filled churches to capacity, seeking penance, or forgiveness, before going to meet their Maker.

Since the northern lights are powered by the sun, changes in solar activity naturally affect auroral displays. Scientists have discovered that the sun follows a cycle of activity that repeats itself about every 11 years. The number of sunspots, and the solar flares (sudden, short-lived explosions) that accompany them, increases each year until the cycle reaches its peak, called solar maximum. The more sunspots there are, the more flares explode, blowing massive amounts of solar particles toward Earth. These incoming particles cause the auroral oval to widen and spread toward the equator, creating large, spectacular displays far from the usual viewing areas.

The most recent solar maximum occurred in 2001. Solar activity was so great that year that the northern lights could be seen as far south as Mexico. Because they're triggered by gusty solar winds, auroral displays during solar maximum are dramatic but short-lived. More consistently brilliant auroras actually occur in the years just before and just after solar maximum. After roughly a year, the number of sunspots slowly begins to decrease, shrinking the auroral oval and returning Earth's magnetic field to a calmer state. The next year of peak solar activity should be 2012.

Intense auroral displays are exciting to watch, but the solar particles that trigger them can also cause a number of problems on Earth. Electric currents caused by dramatic changes in the planet's magnetic field can overload power lines, interfere with

They may be breath-taking, but intense northern lights displays can signal problems for communications systems on Earth. Large amounts of incoming solar particles generate high levels of electricity in the atmosphere, which can overload power lines and interfere with radio and television signals.

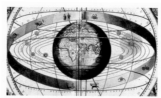

Sounding rockets usually measure 35 to 65 feet (11–20 m) long and are divided into two parts: the motor and the payload (the instruments used to collect data). Once its fuel is spent, the motor separates, but the payload continues into space until all experiments are completed. Total rocket flight time is typically less than 30 minutes.

television signals, disrupt radio and telephone communications, and even damage orbiting satellites. In 1989, violent solar activity knocked out a Canadian power station, leaving six million people without electricity for nine hours. Sudden changes in the magnetic field can also cause electric currents to flow through gas pipelines, leading to **corrosion**.

Auroral researchers today launch satellites into space to study the sun, Earth's magnetic field, and aurora creation both here on Earth and on other planets. Poker Flat Research Range, near Fairbanks, Alaska, has launched hundreds of **sounding rockets** into the northern lights since 1969 to study the aurora's affect on the atmosphere. Rockets are useful tools, as they gather data that's too high for research balloons and too low for

orbiting satellites. Some scientists believe that in the future it may be possible to harness the power of the northern lights, but that reality is still many, many years away.

Arguably the world's most mesmerizing natural wonder, the northern lights have flickered and jumped, rippled and swayed across the sky since long before the first humans walked the earth. Called "merry dancers," "fox fire," "flying dragons," and "swords in heaven," they have comforted some cultures and terrified others. But no matter what name people give them, or how much scientific data we collect about their formation, the northern lights will forever have the power to turn our faces skyward and spark our imagination.

Sounding rockets are one of the best tools available for today's auroral researchers, as they can be launched directly into an aurora, allowing scientists to study it from the inside. Poker Flat Research Range, in Fairbanks, Alaska, is the only high-latitude, auroral-zone rocket launching facility in the U.S.

SEEING THE WONDER

The remote Alaskan countryside (opposite), far from any artificial sources of light, offers observers in North America the best place from which to view the northern lights. In Europe, Iceland and northern Scandinavia are prime viewing locations.

One of the best places from which to view the northern lights is Fairbanks, Alaska, as it's easily accessible and usually lies directly below the auroral oval. Even though the aurora shines every day of the year, light displays appear most frequently in the period between late September and early April because the days are shorter, meaning the sky stays darker longer.

For best viewing, choose a clear, moonless night. Move away from all artificial light. Once you've found a good viewing spot, give your eyes about 20 minutes to adjust to the dark and then look to the northeast. Auroral activity usually peaks around midnight, but auroras can appear as early as twilight or as late as just before dawn. The difference between clouds and the northern lights is that the lights will show signs of movement and may rapidly change shape. While many colors are possible, green appears most often.

Taking photographs of the aurora can be challenging. You must use a tripod to keep your camera still. Any movement will blur the image. Because the

Very few sunspots were observed from about 1645 to 1715. Consequently, the number of auroras at that time dropped dramatically. Known today as the Maunder minimum, after solar astronomer E. W. Maunder, this period coincided with very cold winters in Europe. Scientists are still debating whether the two events are related.

light of the aurora is very faint, the camera's lens will need to be open from 1 to 20 seconds to take in enough light to imprint an image on the film. Because of this, a manually adjustable camera, as opposed to an automatic or disposable one, is ideal. Film coded ASA200 or ASA400 works best. Make sure the flash is turned off.

Northern lights displays cannot be guaranteed, but you can increase your chances of seeing the lights by consulting an auroral prediction service such as the Space Environment Center in Boulder, Colorado, before you go. Researchers there provide updates on solar activity and disturbances in Earth's magnetic field and can usually predict displays up to three days in advance. Call (303) 497-3235 for a recorded message, updated four times a day, or log on to http://www.sel.noaa.gov/pmap/index.html for more detailed viewing information. But remember: cloud cover, city lights, and your location can all affect your chances of seeing a light show. The aurora can be fickle. You may need to watch the skies for many nights before seeing anything. Just be observant, patient, and warmly dressed!

Whether viewed through telescopes or with the naked eye, auroras will always be a source of fascination for people around the world.

NORTHERN  LIGHTS

QUICK FACTS

Cause: The collision of solar particles with gases in Earth's atmosphere

Elevation: Bottom edge is about 60 miles (97 km) above the earth; upper edge may extend to 620 miles (1,000 km)

Best viewing spots: Northernmost regions of the world, including Alaska, Canada, Nordic countries (Finland, Norway, Sweden), Greenland, Iceland, and northern Russia

Best viewing time of year: Clear nights in late autumn or early spring

Best viewing time of day: Midnight

Most common color: Yellow-green

Most common shapes: Arcs, bands, rays, and curtains

Most common sounds: Alleged "swishing" or "crackling" sounds; neither has been officially recorded nor scientifically proven to exist

First useful photograph: A black-and-white photo taken by Martin Brendel in 1892

Notable auroral researchers: Norwegian Kristian Birkeland, widely considered the "father of modern auroral science"; Swedish physicist Hannes Alfvén, who received the Nobel Prize in Physics in 1970

Notable auroral research range: Poker Flat Research Range (Fairbanks, AK), the largest land-based rocket range in the world

Other names: *Aurora borealis*, a term coined by Galileo Galilei in 1616, which means "northern dawn"; *aurora polaris*, or "polar lights," is a general name for both the northern lights and the southern lights (also known as *aurora australis*)

apocalypse—the sudden and violent end of the world as foretold in various religious texts

atmosphere—the layers of air (gases) above the earth; Earth's atmosphere consists mainly of oxygen and nitrogen

aurora—light emitted when solar particles collide with atmospheric gases; northern auroras are called the *aurora borealis*

celestial—related to the sky or universe; the planets, moon, and stars are examples of celestial objects

corrosion—the gradual wearing away of something; the rusting of iron is an example of corrosion

electrons—electrically charged atom particles; electrons swirl around an atom's center, which is made of tightly bound particles called protons and neutrons

geomagnetic north pole—the point on Earth's northern hemisphere where the planet's magnetic pull is strongest

indigenous—races or species that are native to, or have originated in, a particular region

Inuit—indigenous peoples of northern North America who live across Canada, Greenland, Alaska, and the northeastern tip of Asia; also called Eskimos

magnetic field—an invisible area around a magnet within which the magnet's pull can be felt

molecules—two or more atoms of the same kind (such as the oxygen molecule, O_2) or different kinds (such as the salt molecule, NaCl) joined together

sounding rockets—rockets used in scientific research to obtain atmospheric data; to "sound" means to measure

sunspots—relatively cool areas on the sun's surface that appear as dark spots; sunspots are a measure of solar activity

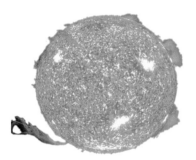